Birthday Parties & Cakes for Kids

pil
Publications International, Ltd.

Writer: Lynda Twardowski is a freelance writer who specializes in the child and teen market. She is the author of *Face Facts: How to Bring Out the Beautiful You,* and her articles have appeared in a variety of magazines and Web sites, including *Teen Style, All About You!,* KidsHealth.org, and PlanetGirl.com.

Crafter: Phyllis Dunstan

Photography: Sanders Studios, Inc., Silver Lining Digital, Inc.
Food Stylists: Carol Parik, Teri Rys-Maki
Photo Stylists: Ana M. Gonzalez, Kathy Lapin
Additional Photography: Siede/Preis Photography, Brian Warling Photography

Pictured on the front cover *(clockwise from top left):* Picasso's Palate *(page 21),* Sweet Victory *(page 95)* and Microphone Mania *(page 66).*
Pictured on the back cover: Out of This World *(page 14).*

Contents

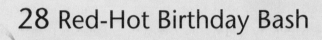

Planning a Perfect Party

What's more exciting for a child than the thought of a party—especially their very own birthday party! And the thought is pretty exciting for you, too. That is, until you start worrying about how to throw the perfect party—without a lot of work, headaches, or expense.

That's where *Birthday Parties & Cakes for Kids* comes in! With this book in hand, you can plan the perfect party with minimal muss and even less fuss. Simple, homemade birthday parties are just as exciting and far more special than any you could order by phone. Not only can you tailor the party to your guest of honor, you can increase your child's anticipation of the big event by inviting him or her to help you create the invitations, plan the activities, decorate the house, pick out game prizes and favors, and bake the

cake. Most of the parties require minimal effort and not much more than your average house-hold trappings; a few require a simple trip to the local craft, party, or hardware store. None require you to dip into your child's college education fund!

Timing is everything

Generally, birthday parties work best in the early afternoon. Younger kids (ages 4 to 6) tend to get cranky by the end of the day, and older kids (ages 7 to 10) tend to get hungry. If you're serving a meal along with birth-day cake and ice cream, that won't be a problem, but if picky eaters and food allergies run rampant on your guest list, you might want to plan your party to avoid mealtimes.

Most important, however, is how long the party runs. Many parents find that 90 minutes is

enough time to feed and entertain a group of young partygoers (trusting the "get 'em going while the going's still good" theory of party hosting). But if the kids are eight and older and you have some interesting activities planned, a two- to three-hour event may be worth considering.

However you schedule the party, be sure to note the event's start and end times, as well as meal plans, on the invitation so your guests and their parents know what to expect. Mail or hand-deliver invitations two to three weeks before the party. Request an RSVP instead of 'regrets only' so you can be sure all the invitees received the invitation.

Table for...?

A common rule of thumb is to plan the guest list based on the birthday child's age plus one: five guests for a 4-year-old, ten for a 9-year-old, etc. This rule serves parents well and makes each passing year increasingly special for the birthday boy or girl. To avoid snubs or hurt feelings, many parents choose to invite the child's entire school class, or at least all the kids of the child's gender. Do what you're comfortable with—just make sure you enlist plenty of help to supervise a big party.

Age is much more than a number

The key to throwing a great party is understanding the age of those on the guest list.

4-year-olds: Thanks to day care and preschool, most kids this age are at ease in social situations and are eager to take part in activities like singing, coloring, or simple games. Some may need a little more coaxing. For kids in this age group, make it clear that parents are encouraged to stay for the party. Have some adult finger foods on hand.

5-year-olds: This is one of the best ages for a party! Five-year-olds tend to be fairly independent, and they put a lot of heart into whatever is going on around them. They respond well to organized activities and attack simple skill games with gusto.

6-year-olds: Kids are a little more competitive and rambunctious at this age. Ward off hurt feelings by offering both winner and participants prizes for the games.

7- and 8-year-olds: Giggle central! Kids in this age group tend to blend well among the sexes, but you may hear the first requests for "girls only!" or "no girls allowed!" Let your child determine the guest list. No matter who's there, these kids love to crack jokes, get silly, and laugh at just about anything. Inspire them with goofy activities like fill-in-the-blank word games and high-energy games such as relay races and tag.

9- and 10-year-olds: Maturity has officially set in—or so the kids believe. Children this age can be very particular, so let the birthday child take the reins in planning the party. Decorations, menu, and games will be chosen with a discerning eye. Make sure no one's left out by organizing team-oriented games such as a scavenger hunt or low-key group activities. Slumber parties are great for this age!

Put "extra" in the extraordinary

Above all, your child's party should be safe, simple, and special. And that's precisely why a homemade party is so wonderful: because you—not a sports club employee or pizza parlor pro—are the magician making your child's wishes come true.

To keep things safe, merely think like a parent: Clear the party zone of breakable, dangerous, or messy items. Put tape over the bathroom door lock so little ones don't accidentally lock themselves in. To ensure young kids make it there in time, run a ribbon or cutout arrows along the hallway floor leading to the bathroom. Shut doors to rooms that are off-limits, or tape streamers or birthday signs across doorless entryways to prevent kids from wandering out of bounds.

To keep the party simple, designate one room for games and presents, another for food and crafts.

If you can host any part of the party outdoors, do! Kids love the festive feel of a picnic, and you'll love using a hose to clean up. However, even if sunshine is predicted, don't trust the forecast completely; have a backup plan ready in case of rain. Also, streamers and poster board bleed when wet, so consider Mylar balloons, plastic lawn flowers, or plastic banners for outdoor events, just in case.

Once you've got safety and simplicity in the bag, it's time to make this birthday bash the most special ever. Establish an extraordinary aura early by decorating the entrance to the party with balloons, streamers, or Christmas lights. Everyone will feel the excitement of the party zone. Plan a low-key activity the kids can dive into one by one, as soon as they arrive, to help them feel comfortable immediately.

Add flourishes and personal touches whenever possible. Keep fidgeting to a minimum during serving time by covering the table with butcher paper and placing crayons at each place. Small toys and paper cups filled with treats work great, too. Taking pictures of the birthday child with each guest; bestowing each guest with a crown or "special" slice of cake—any one of these small efforts goes a long way toward delighting your guests and making wonderful memories for your child.

And really, isn't that what birthday parties are all about?

Space Out

There comes a time in every parent's life (usually when they peek into the black hole that is their offspring's bedroom) when they wonder: "Is my child an alien?" For this birthday, the answer should be a resounding, "Yes!" Honor your favorite space cadet by launching a birthday blast that's out of this world. With these simple tricks and crafts, Houston, it'll be no problem.

INVITATIONS

Rocket Mail

In the weeks before the party, save, and enlist your friends to save, empty toilet paper rolls. (You'll need one for each child on the guest list.) Follow these simple steps to make stellar rocket invitations.

1. Cover each cardboard roll with colored construction paper, and glue in place. Trim excess paper.
2. Trace around a CD onto colored construction paper, and cut out 1 circle for each party invitation.
3. Roll each circle into a cone. Secure with tape.

SPACE OUT!
Join us on our mission to celebrate Jen's birthday! Shuttle over to Planet Hughes, 1234 Maple Lane, for a launch lunch, games, and fun! RSVP 555-1234.
Liftoff: 11:00 Sat., Oct. 5
Return to Earth: 1:00
It's one small year for Jen, one giant party for Jen's birthday!

(continued on page 10)

(continued from page 8)

4. Tape a cone to the top of each cardboard roll.

5. Cut yellow, red, or orange construction paper (1 piece for every 2 invitations) in half, and write the details of the party on each piece, leaving an inch blank at the bottom.

6. Cut small vertical slits into the bottom of each invitation to create a fringe.

7. Roll up the paper and slide it inside the cardboard tube, with the fringe sticking out of the bottom. Use a pencil to curl the fringe for a hot "flame" effect.

8. Decorate the outside of the rockets with stickers or markers before launching them into the guests' hands.

DECORATIONS

Put Your Best Space Forward

Turning your home into the moon is as easy as 3–2–1. Stretch cotton batting (found at craft or sewing stores) over the floor and furniture to make your home look like the surface of the moon, then twist a black lightbulb into a ceiling fixture or lamp, and—voilà!—you're lost in space!

To really get glowing, cut a few stars out of cardboard or poster board, wrap them in aluminum foil, and suspend them from the ceiling with black string; or hang glow-in-the-dark stars and planets. (Warning, Commander: Young kids may be scared of the dark and prefer a walk on the moon that's lit more like the sun.) For out-of-this-world music, try playing the sound-tracks from *Star Wars, Close Encounters of the Third Kind,* or *2001: A Space Odyssey* as background music.

Jet Pack Activity

In the weeks before the party, round up 1 old shoe box, with lid, for each guest. Poke 4 holes in the bottom of each box (1 in each corner). Wrap the box and the lid with aluminum foil. Push pieces of elastic through the holes in the back of each box to make them look like backpacks. Knot the ends of the elastic on the inside of the box so they won't pull through the holes. Glue the lid to the top of the box. Cut colored construction paper or shiny foil wrapping paper into dozens of different shapes.

When the kids arrive, set out the shapes as well as crayons or markers, glitter, foam shapes, paper cups, colored yarn or string, and plenty of tape and craft glue. Let the kids personalize their packs however they want. And don't worry about the mess. Let it fall on the cotton batting, and when the kids finish, just roll the whole thing up and toss it out!

Mission to the Moon

Before the party, cut out and paste a yellow moon in the center of a piece of blue poster

board, and surround it with pictures of planets as well as black holes and asteroids.

Lay the game board flat, and invite each child to toss a small beanbag or stuffed toy (dress it in an aluminum-foil space suit!) from across the room to the moon. Allow each child a turn until he or she has made it. For older kids, assign a point system to the solar system, and allow each guest three tosses.

If weather permits, go outside and let kids launch a mission to the moon with a foot pump rocket (find them at toy stores or in the toy section at the supermarket) instead of—or in addition to—a toss.

If Kids Could Save Time in a Capsule

For futuristic fun, create a time capsule. Take a picture of each child and ask them what they want to be when they grow up; what their favorite TV show is; and what they like best about being their age. Write the answers on the back of their picture with a felt-tip pen. Drop their pictures into an airtight jar or tube, along with a news-paper clipping and anything else that commemorates the special day for the birthday host. (Try an empty tennis ball tube, and seal it in a resealable plastic storage bag.) With your help, the kids can bury the capsule in the yard. Invite them back for next year's—or next decade's—birthday unearthing.

Launchtime

Crumb-free, freeze-dried food is the rule in space—so why not let the kids test their taste buds on the same fare? Find inexpen-sive and delicious dehydrated meals at camping supply stores. Choose uncomplicated fare like spaghetti, macaroni and cheese, or chicken-and-rice meals. Stock up on a small smorgasbord, and let the astronauts pick their meal pack. All you need to do is add hot water, stir, wait, and serve.

The guests can wash the meal down with a nice big cup of Tang. Here's another idea: Make glowing planets or asteroids by freezing Tang in ball-shape ice trays in the days before the party. Serve the ice balls in glasses of clear soda garnished with tiny American flags.

12

Moon Rocks

*Easy-to-make popcorn balls make for great edible
planets or "moon rocks."*

2⅝ cups powdered sugar
1 cup marshmallows
¾ cup light corn syrup
¼ cup margarine
2 teaspoons cold water
5 quarts *popped* popcorn
Vegetable shortening

1. Combine powdered sugar, marshmallows, corn syrup,
margarine, and water in a saucepan. Bring to a boil over
medium heat, stirring constantly.

2. Place popped popcorn in large bowl; toss with corn syrup
mixture until popcorn is evenly coated.

3. Grease hands with vegetable shortening; quickly shape
coated popcorn into balls. Place on waxed paper to cool.

4. Wrap in plastic wrap until ready to use.

Makes approximately 2 dozen popcorn balls

Out of This World

Want to really wow your earthling guests?
Serve up a UFO cake.

4½ cups cake batter, divided
1 (10-inch) round cake board, covered, or large plate
1¾ cups prepared white frosting
    Food coloring
    Red decorator gel
    Black licorice twists
8 to 10 large gumballs
    Assorted candies

I. Preheat oven to 350°F. Grease and flour 9-inch round cake pan and 1½ quart ovenproof bowl. Pour 2¾ cups cake batter into prepared cake pan; pour 1¾ cups cake batter into prepared bowl. Bake cake in pan 30 to 35 minutes and cake in bowl 45 to 55 minutes or until wooden skewer inserted into centers comes out clean. Cool 15 minutes in pans. Loosen edges; invert onto wire racks and cool completely.

2. Trim top of bowl cake and top and side of round cake. Place round cake on prepared cake board. Spread small amount of frosting on center of round cake. Place bowl cake, flat side down, on top of round cake.

3. Reserve ¼ cup frosting; tint remaining 1½ cups frosting blue-gray.

4. Frost entire cake with blue-gray frosting. Frost top half of bowl cake with white frosting (over blue-gray frosting). Cover top of bowl cake with red decorator gel (over white frosting).

5. Cut licorice twists into 1½-inch pieces; arrange on bowl cake as shown in photo. Decorate UFO with gumballs and assorted candies as shown in photo.

Makes 12 to 14 servings

Shuttle Scuttle

Fill fun containers or bags with space-age goodies: mini flash-lights, Milky Way candy bars, glow-in-the-dark super balls, star or planet stickers, glow sticks, small American flags, and freeze-dried astronaut ice cream (available at camping stores).

You Gotta Have Art

Crack open some creativity, and paint a party your kid will never forget! Worried you're not crafty enough? No sweat. We've provided all the inspiration you'll need to make your grand artistic vision a reality. Just grab some color and canvas; the kids will be happy to provide the rest.

INVITATIONS

Inspired Invitations

Color your guests invited by sending them invitations shaped like an artist's palette.

1. Draw a palette shape on white poster board or construction paper, and cut out.

2. For paint puddles, cut different colors of construction paper into freeform shapes about twice the size of a silver dollar. Inside each paint puddle, write a particular about the party.

3. Cut an oval about half the size of the paint puddles out of black construction paper.

4. Glue the oval and paint puddles around the palette.

Join us Saturday October 5

11:00-1:00 at Sally's art studio

1234 Maple Lane

It's Sally's 6th birthday, and we're painting the town!

Lunch, cake, & ice cream will be served.

Bring your creativity and a smock!

RSVP 555-1234

White Space

A well-lit workspace is key to any art studio. Turn your party room into a worthy workroom by clearing out as much furniture as possible, cranking up the lights, and yanking up the blinds. Cover the floor with a large tarp, either paper or canvas. If you can't wait for the kids to leave their marks, let the birthday girl or boy have some pre-party fun by splattering the canvas with different color paints a few days before the event so the paint splatters have time to dry.

Set out folding chairs to be used as easels, one per guest. Clip a sheet of white paper to a larger piece of stiff cardboard (if you're providing watercolor paints) or inexpensive particle board (if the kids will be drawing with crayons or markers).

For younger kids, try washable finger paints and white poster board, and skip the paper and board backing. Whichever "canvas" you choose, prop it up against the chair's back so it will stay steady as the kids work. On each chair seat, set out paper towels, paints and brushes, or markers. It's a good idea to put the same equipment at each place. This minimizes the threat of the kids wandering around with dripping paintbrushes, looking for other supplies.

Although kids rarely need any more inspiration than their own imagination, an unbreakable vase filled with flowers, a bowl of fruit, or even a posed doll can be set out for use as subjects for a still-life painting.

Art-eests' Aura

To lend even more ambience, elevate the kids from artists to "art-eests" by playing a cool French CD, such as one by famed French crooner Edith Piaf, and offering the kids painter berets to wear.

Party Arty

For guests who really want to get their hands dirty—and

parents who want to keep things clean—there's no better deal than salt clay. Mix some up the day before the party, and keep it covered in the fridge until the kids are ready to sculpt. To make it, knead 2 cups all-purpose flour, 1 cup salt, and 1 cup water together. For colored clay, add a couple drops of food coloring to the water before adding it to the flour. Estimate 1 batch for every 2 kids. (Remind the kids to let their sculptures air-dry overnight!)

For more party fun, try these creative games:

• **Back to the drawing board:** Kids will love this drawing challenge. Before the party, write different words or phrases on index cards. Try to make the level of difficulty appropriate to the age group. (Words and phrases like "touchdown," "birdhouse," "bedtime," "tickled pink," or "dog pound" are good starters.) At the party, have each artist take a turn pulling one of the cards from the stack you've created. Without speaking the word or phrase on his card, the artist must communicate the word to the other kids by drawing. Use a chalkboard, a wet- or dry-erase board, or a large piece of paper taped to the wall. Or, up the excitement by having them use salt clay instead of a drawing board.

• **Artist directs:** Draw a few silly faces with unusual features, such as a smile that starts as a frown, one fat ear up high and one skinny ear down low, etc. Show a face to all but one artist, who is blindfolded. As the other children watch, let one child describe the silly face to the artist, directing him to draw what she is describing. The crazier the faces, the louder the giggles!

Above: *Add a splash of color to the party with this fabulous palette cake;* **Left:** *Personal pizzas become works of art when the guests display their creativity. And who knows? They may even be inspired to eat their vegetables!*

Picasso's Palette

*Follow up with a cake that's easier than
painting by numbers.*

1 (9-inch) round cake
1 (10-inch) round cake board, covered, or large plate
1 cup prepared white frosting
 Assorted-color decorator gels and food coloring
 Red pull-apart licorice twist
1 pretzel rod

1. Trim top and side of cake. Cut out small circle on one side of cake; cut piece from side of cake to create palette shape as shown in photo. Place on prepared cake board.

2. Tint frosting light brown.

3. Frost entire cake with brown frosting.

4. Pipe spots of paint on palette with decorator gels.

5. Create artist's paintbrush by cutting 2-inch lengths of licorice and connecting them to pretzel rod with foil as shown in photo.

Makes 10 to 12 servings

Personal Pizzas

Before the kids get started on their paintings, jump-start their creativity by spreading a palette of colorful pizza toppings before them (tomatoes, green peppers, black olives, yellow banana peppers, cheese, etc.) and letting them design their own personal pizzas. While the pizzas are in the oven, keep the guests busy painting in the other room.

Supplies Surprise

Send the salt-clay sculptures home with the guests as part of their goodie bag haul—a painter's apron or sack packed with inexpensive art supplies like paintbrushes, a small paint set, crayons, gel pens, glitter, or glue sticks.

Glamorama

Your little girl is growing up, and you don't want to miss a minute. This year, set aside a couple hours to watch as she and her pals dabble in the big girl world. You provide the tools, the encouragement, and a camera to capture it all, and it's guaranteed: They'll provide plenty of entertainment.

INVITATIONS

Compact Invitation

Decorate hot pink or purple poster board for invitations as glamorous as the party.

1. For each invitation, trace around a small, round container twice, drawing 2 circles next to each other with the edges touching.

2. Cut out the pair as 1 piece, taking care not to slice the area where they meet. Fold the circles one on top of the other, like a pressed-powder compact.

3. Write the party particulars on the inside of the compact.

4. Cut out a small circle of aluminum foil to serve as the mirror, and glue it inside the top circle. Decorate with stickers.

Sparkle Shimmer and Shine Taylor's turning nine! Come to Taylor's Glamorama birthday party. Noon to 2:00 p.m. Saturday, October 5 (No need to be fashionably late.)

(continued on page 24)

(continued from page 22)

5. Personalize the top of the compact with stickers or a fancy drawing by the birthday girl, or write each invitee's name in fancy script with silver or sparkly ink. Voilà! Trēs magnifique!

DECORATIONS

Think Pink

Or, more accurately, think whatever color your princess-for-a-day would like to use for her "signature color." Streamers, balloons, and fresh flowers in the chosen color will keep the festivities feminine and fun.

Create a beauty parlor atmosphere with a sign on the door that reads, "(Birthday Girl's name)'s Beauty Parlor" and another in the window that declares this party "Open" for business.

Set up a row of chairs in front of a bathroom mirror or a full-length mirror set on its side. A few weeks before the party, determine the pampering treatments so you have adequate time to gather the necessary tools and ingredients. Make inexpensive and simple moisturizing masks from oatmeal and honey; slice cucumbers to plant on "tired" eyes, or merely set out some makeup and watch them paint away the hours.

One warning: Doin' a 'do can be a lot of fun, but keep in mind that chaos and curling irons don't mix well at any age. Consider limiting hairdressings to fun bows, barrettes, braids, and ponytails.

GAMES/ACTIVITIES

Gossip Game

While the girls are sitting around the table, whisper a silly sentence like, "I love to pick daffodils while wearing red boots" in the ear of one girl, then tell her to pass it on. No one can ask to hear it again or for clarification. Each girl must say exactly what she thinks she heard the first time. That way, the end result is usually a laughable lump of gossip akin to, "Eloise is sick of Ralph O'Dell, the crazy old coot."

Model Behavior

While you've got the gals gussied up, invite them to pose for pictures. Or, if you've got a video camera on hand and they're ready to strut their stuff, let them organize a fashion show to music. You're the videographer!

Fill-in-the-Blank Word Game Madness

Ladies may lunch, but real girls get goofy. Help out by preparing a silly story or two about the birthday girl before the party. For example,

"Taylor had it made. She was finally ___ years old! To celebrate, she jumped into a car made of _____ and trucked to the nearest _____ stand. She asked the guy behind the counter, Farmer _____, what was for breakfast. He said he'd sell her two _____ for a dollar."

Without reading the story to the kids, ask them to give you a word for each of the following: 1) number; 2) noun; 3) food; 4) boy's name; 5) plural noun.

Obviously, the answers may get quite silly and so may the girls. They'll enjoy every minute of it, and so will you.

Pre-Party Craft

Spend some quality time with your birthday girl before the party making special gifts for the guests. One idea? Home-made body glitter. Mix 1 cup clear aloe vera gel with 1 teaspoon glycerin, then add 1 teaspoon fine polyester glitter. Add a drop of fragrance oil and/or food coloring if you'd like, stir, and then spoon the sparkly gel into small jars (find them at craft stores). Personalize the jars with stickers or hand-colored labels, and drop them in the guests' goodie bags.

REFRESHMENTS

Spa Snacks

Go for extreme glamour with jewel-colored hard candies, a tray of cheese and crackers, finger sand-wiches, exotic fruits on plastic skewers, fancy chocolates. You can find inexpen-sive, ornate serving platters and dishes at party stores and dollar stores.

FAVORS

Beauty Bag

Before the beauties rush off, make sure they're prepared for bad hair days and social engagements by handing them a pretty gift bag that includes candy rings and necklaces, petite nail polish samples, sunglasses, a cute plastic comb or hairbrush, and fun hair doodads like clips, barrettes, and bows.

Beauty Treat

At the end of a hard day's pampering, drained divas absolutely must recharge with a slice of the good life. With a dress dripping in rich frosting, there's nothing sweeter than this cake.

5½ cups cake batter, divided
1 (10-inch) round prepared cake board, covered, or large plate
2 cans (16 ounces each) white frosting
Food coloring
1 doll
Assorted candies and decors

1. Preheat oven to 350°F. Grease and flour 2-quart ovenproof bowl and 8-inch round cake pan. Pour 3½ cups cake batter into prepared bowl; pour 2 cups cake batter into cake pan. Bake cake in bowl 55 to 60 minutes and cake in pan 25 to 30 minutes or until wooden skewer inserted into centers comes out clean. Cool 15 minutes in pans. Loosen edges; invert onto wire racks and cool completely.

2. Trim flat side of bowl cake. Trim side of round cake so edge is even with bowl cake. Place round cake on prepared cake board.

3. Frost top of round cake lightly with frosting. Place bowl cake, flat side down, on top of round cake.

4. Tint 1 cup frosting purple and remaining frosting pink.

5. Frost entire cake with pink frosting.

6. Make small cut in center of cake, and insert doll into cake. (To keep doll's clothing clean, first wrap bottom of doll in plastic wrap.)

7. Using medium writing tip and purple frosting, pipe designs on party dress. Decorate with assorted candies and decors as shown in photo.   *Makes 14 to 18 servings*

Red-Hot Birthday Bash

Your child has been waiting all year for a five-alarm birthday party, so fan the flames and throw one—with all the bells, whistles, and sirens a firefighter-in-training deserves. A little planning and preparation are all the fuel you'll need to pull off this easy and inexpensive party. Ready? Set? Fire it up!

INVITATIONS

Waterworks

Purchase black plumber hose and water jet nozzles at any hardware store. (You'll need one 6-inch section of hose and 1 nozzle for each invitation.)

1. Spray-paint the nozzle gold or silver. Let dry, then glue it onto the end of a 6-inch length of hose.
2. Cut blue construction paper (1 piece for every 2 invitations) in half, and write the party particulars on each piece, leaving an inch blank at the bottom.
3. Cut small vertical slits into the bottom of each invitation.

Fire it up: Matt is turning 5! Truck on over to 1234 Maple Lane Saturday, October 2, to help him celebrate. The party will burn from 2:00 to 4:00 Expect red-hot games and cool ice cream and cake! RSVP 555-1234

(continued on page 30)

multicolor will do if that's all you've got handy. Think twice before playing a CD with siren noises or providing siren noise-makers; they're harmless in the store but can hand out killer headaches at home.

(continued from page 28)
4. Roll up the paper, and slide it inside the hose with the fringe sticking out the bottom. Use a pencil to curl the fringe so it looks like water is spraying out.
5. Glue a few long strips of blue construction paper to the nozzle as well.
6. Hand-deliver the hoses.

DECORATIONS

Firehouse Rock
Hang cutout flames or red, orange, and yellow streamers over heating vents or near windows for a flapping, flame dance effect. Hot, hot, hot! Set out toy fire trucks and plastic firefighter hats everywhere to set the scene. Blinking red or white Christmas lights around the ceiling are wonderful, but

GAMES/ACTIVITIES

Guest Star
Local firehouses may be happy to send a firefighter over for a free fire safety lesson (carefully masked as the tales of courage and bravery that kids love to hear). Just be sure to book your speaker well in advance of the planned date, and call to con-firm a few days before. Also, ask about coloring books, sticker "badges," and plastic helmets the station likely has on hand.

Hot, Hot, Hot
• If the weather's warm, soak up some super fun with a water balloon toss. Pair kids up so each has a partner. Have an odd number of guests? Create a triangle, or—gulp!—stand in as somebody's partner. Good luck!
• Line kids up next to an unhooked garden hose. Push a marble into one end, and then let kids try to lift, wiggle, and jiggle the hose to get the mar-

ble out the other end. It sounds easier than it looks, and it looks sillier than it sounds.

• Organize a game of tug-o-war for your little firefighters using a garden hose. As their hands sweat, the hose gets slippery!

Emergency Celebration

If the kids are stranded indoors, don't worry; there's still plenty to do. Consider...

• a game of stomp. Stop, drop, and roll is the rule for real fires, but for pretend ones, stomp, stomp, stomp is the way to go. Give guests a chance to perfect their stomping skills by tying a small, inflated balloon to each child's ankle. The kids try to pop each others' balloons by stomping them—without getting their own balloon popped in the process! The last child with an inflated balloon wins.

• an indoor relay race. At one end of the room, set out two chairs with a bowl of water on each. At the other end, place two clear plastic cups marked with a line about an inch from the bottom. Divide the guests into two teams. On "Go," each team sends a player hurrying to their respective bowl with a teaspoon. The job is to scoop out a spoonful of water, walk carefully back to the cup to dump in the water, then pass the empty spoon to the next teammate to repeat. The first group to fill their cup to the mark wins.

Hats Off

Pick up plastic fire helmets from the toy store to use as goodie holders. Label each hat with the guest's name, and fill each overturned hat with firehouse coloring books, a toy firefighter's badge, mini American flags, Red Hots, and Atomic FireBall candies.

31

Where's the Fire?

Race to the birthday scene with this cake, and you'll never hear the wail of a hungry child again. Or, at least not for a few blessed hours, anyway!

1 (13×9-inch) cake
1 (14×10-inch) cake board, covered
1½ cans (16 ounces each) white frosting
  Red food coloring
  Black licorice twists
  Red licorice rope
6 chocolate and vanilla sandwich cookies
  Assorted candies

1. Trim top and sides of cake. Cut cake into pieces as shown in Diagram 2 (page 33).

2. Place piece A on prepared cake board. Place piece B on top of piece A as shown in Diagram 1, attaching with small amount of frosting. Set piece C aside for another use.

3. Tint 2 cups frosting red. Frost windshield area with white frosting. Frost remainder of truck with red frosting.

4. Cut licorice twists into pieces; arrange on fire truck to create ladder and bumpers as shown in photo. Arrange licorice rope on top of truck to resemble hose.

5. Position sandwich cookies for wheels. Decorate fire truck with assorted candies as shown in photo.

Makes 16 to 18 servings

Diagram 1

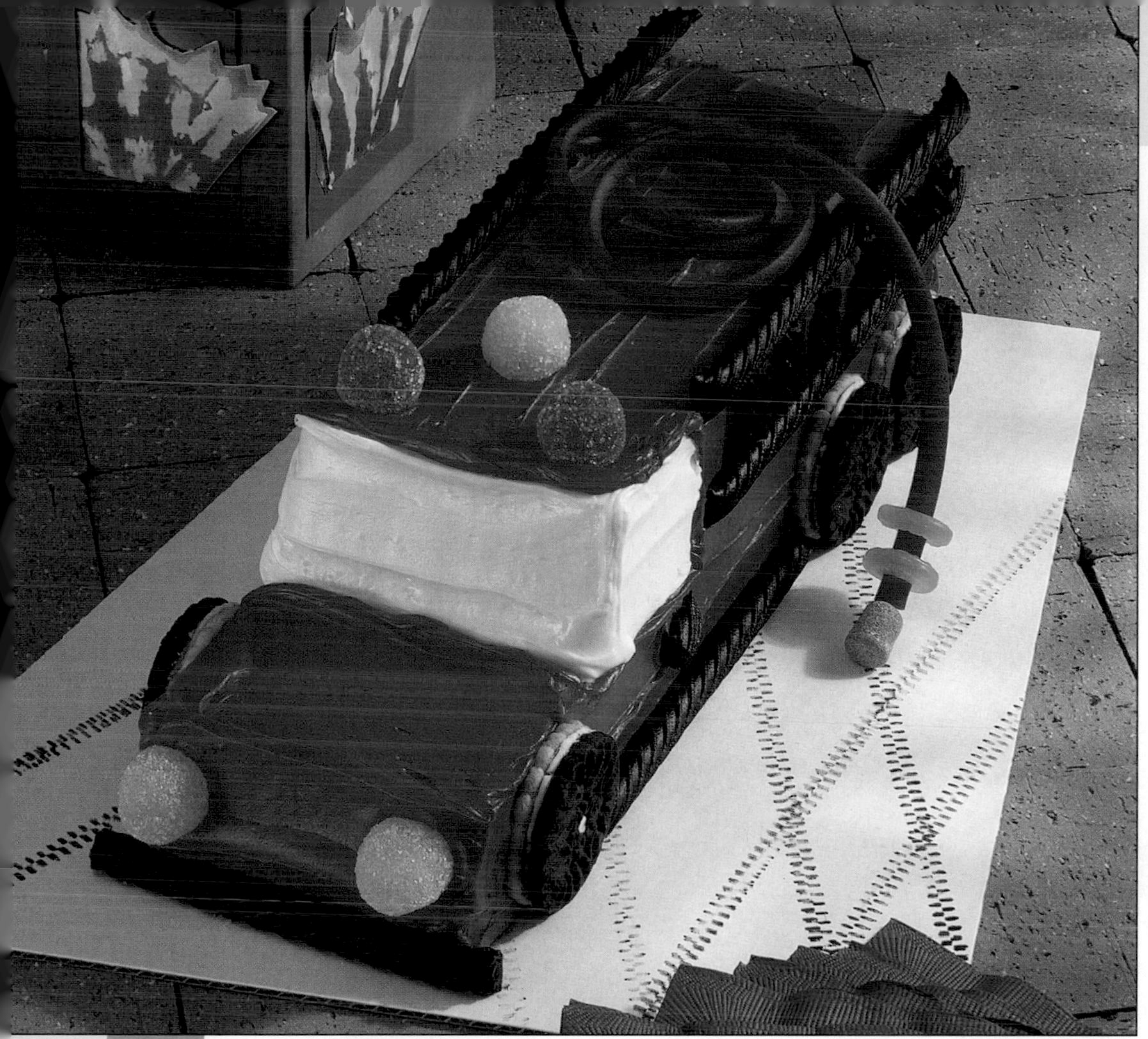

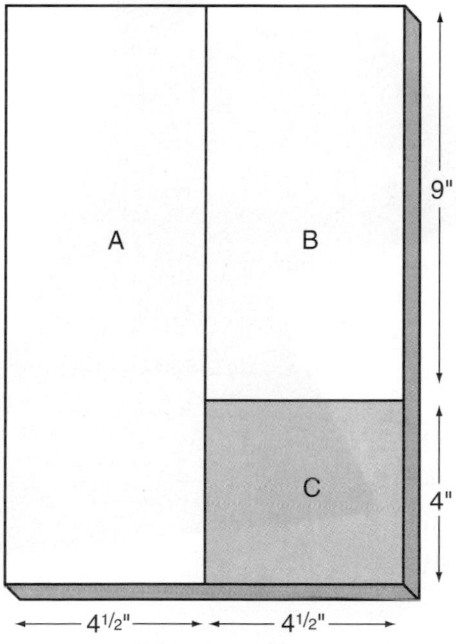

Diagram 2

Cool It

Help kids stay cool in the hot zone by serving lemon-lime soda in clear plastic cups. Drop a few cubes of frozen red fruit punch in each cup, and let the kids stir with straw "hoses." As the cubes begin to melt in their cups, the red will spread out, making a fun flamelike look.

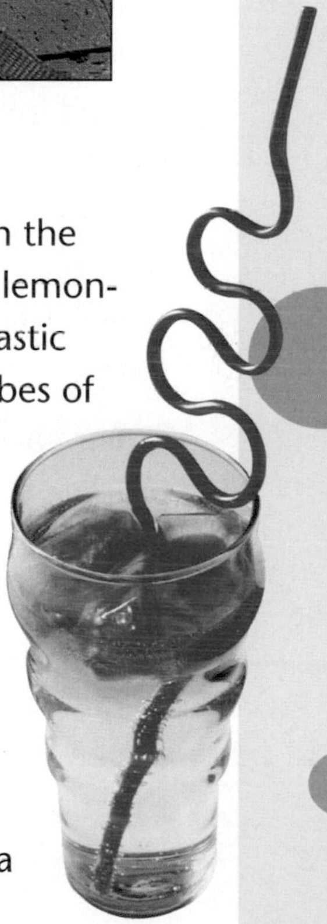

World of Wizards

*F*inding the tail of a dog, eye of newt, and hair from the head of a three-legged goat just isn't as easy as it used to be! But don't let that stop you from concocting a magical birthday for your wonderful wizard. Kids will be spellbound by these easy-to-make invitations, decorations, and delectables.

INVITATIONS

Conjuring the Guests

Is your hex for making people appear a little rusty? Then rely on the magic of mailed invitations to get your guests together. While these invitations may look magical, unfortunately they won't magically deliver them-selves. Mail or hand-deliver them.

1. For each invitation, cut 2 triangles out of black construction paper. Each triangle should be 8 inches high and 5 inches wide at its base.

2. Use stencils or templates to trace star shapes on aluminum foil or construction paper, or draw them freehand and cut them out. (Or, use stickers! Holographic stickers would look especially cool.)

CALLING ALL WIZARDS

Heather is brewing up a birthday party.

Ride your broomstick to 1234 Maple Ln. for a MAGICAL party of wizard games, food & fun!

Saturday, October 5th
11:00 – 1:00
(No owls allowed!)
RSVP to the hex hotline 555-1234.

(continued on page 36)

(continued from page 34)

ß. Glue these shapes onto the front of one of the triangles, and decorate with glitter glue. This is the front of the invitation.

4. On the second triangle, write the party details in silver or gold ink, which shines like lightning on dark paper.

5. Glue or tape the triangles together at the top point only so the card opens from the bottom.

DECORATIONS

Bewitching Decor

Purple, black, and silver balloons are an excellent starting point. For an absolutely magical look, make them hover and float in midair. How? Simply inflate each balloon with a mix of helium and air. If you've got a

guest list of kids who aren't afraid of the dark, draw the curtains shut in the party room, and screw in a black lightbulb.

A bubbling cauldron of dry ice always looks wonderful, but be sure you keep it out of reach in a corner and under your watchful eye; you don't want any curious kids trying to grab hold of the ice. If you'd rather not risk the dry ice, set a broomstick in the corner instead; it's also bewitching.

Spread a purple or black tablecloth on the table, and at each place setting, set a wizard hat. Inexpensive wizard hats are available at most party or craft stores. Or, make your own wizard hats ahead of time by rolling sheets of 11×17-inch paper into cones. Fit each cone on your child's head before taping the 2 sides together. Fold under or trim away the excess paper at the bottom to tidy up the cone's shape. Decorate with foil star stickers before the party, or leave them blank and allow the guests to decorate their hats themselves for a cool project.

FAVORS

Use a shimmery or sparkly sack to hold magical party favors such as magic wands (find colored balloon sticks at your local florist shop, or use glow sticks), tiny spell books (read: colorful miniature notebooks), stickers, and Pop Rocks exploding candy. You may even want to compose a few friendship, love, or study spells for kids to try.

REFRESHMENTS

Bubble, Bubble...

...toil is trouble. For a no-fuss meal, brew up a cauldron of wizard's brew. Simply heat up a few cans of chicken-and-stars soup. Add a special ingredient by slicing up a carrot before the party and cutting each round into a star shape. Let the carrot stars simmer in the soup, and be sure to serve one in each bowl. You can tell the kids that a star appearing in their bowl is the mark of a great wizard.

Sorcerer's Sauce

Give kids a cauldron of their own by pouring warm maple syrup or melted peanut butter (or a mix of both) in small paper cups and letting kids dip slices of apple, banana, strawberries, or other fruits. Make this snack magical by providing a few shakers of candy sprinkles for toppings. Just remember: Truly wise wizard parents will keep kids seated and at a covered table, because these sticky snacks can be messy!

Cast a Sweet Spell

So you've forgotten the words to the spell that seals a child's lips? Don't worry—as long as you have this mouthwatering recipe for Wizard Cake, you'll hear nothing but happy chewing.

1 (13×9-inch) cake
1 (19×13-inch) cake board, cut in half crosswise and
    covered, or large platter
1½ cups prepared white frosting
    Blue food coloring
    Yellow rectangular gummy candies

1. Trim top and sides of cake. Using diagram below as your guide, draw hat pattern on 13×9-inch piece of waxed paper. Cut out pattern, and place on cake. Cut out hat; place on prepared cake board.

2. Tint frosting blue.

3. Frost entire cake with blue frosting.

4. Flatten gummy candies with rolling pin on smooth, flat surface or sheet of waxed paper sprinkled with sugar. Roll until very thin (about ¹⁄₁₆ inch), turning frequently to coat with sugar. Cut out star and crescent shapes with sharp knife or scissors.

5. Arrange stars and crescents on cake as shown in photo.

Makes 12 to 16 servings

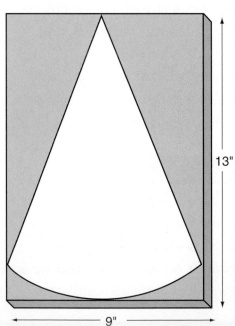

13"

9"

Abracadabra

Should you feel like splurging, hire a magician to entertain the kids. Kids of all ages love to watch magic shows, and best of all, the guests often can get in on the act. Find magicians-for-hire in the phone book, or consider calling local community recreation or college extension programs. Many offer magic classes and may be able to put you in touch with a student or part-time magic teacher whose fee is probably quite a bit more reasonable than that of a professional magician.

Wizard Hunt

Unleash your guests on a scavenger hunt for all the ingredients a young wizard needs nowadays. (For guests too young to be crossing the street, merely hide these ingredients around the house.) Challenge the guests to track down, in one hour (half an hour for young seekers):

• Eye of newt (jelly bean)
• Hair of witch (piece of yarn)
• Magic dust (pinch of glitter)
• Row of snake teeth (grains of white rice)
• Button from an invisible cloak (clear-colored button)
• Kidney of mouse (kidney bean)
• Owl feather (any feather)
• Wish candle (birthday candle)

Reward the winning team with fancy pens or pencils (look for decorative pencils topped with a feather or shoots of cellophane; any sparkly gel pen would also work nicely) to use for writing down their special spells.

Otherworldly Games

If you find that the guests still have energy left to burn, let them burn off their motion

potion fuel with any of these fun games.

• **Warlock walk.** Place an air-filled balloon between the backs of two partners, and have them race other teams across the room. The teams have to coordinate walking together across the room without dropping the balloon (if it touches the floor, they need to go back to the starting point) and releasing it into an open box on the floor. No hands allowed!

• **Grab for apples.** Carve a star shape out of an apple, and fill a clean plastic storage or laundry tub with water and one apple for every wizard. (Remember: Only one apple has the special "mark.") Place the tub on a large towel to catch splashes, and let the kids take turns reach-

ing in, wearing a blindfold or with eyes closed, to grab an apple. Award a prize to the winning wizard who ends up with the special apple.

• **Magical musical chairs.** Another oldie but goodie. Play "We're Off to See the Wizard" from the *Wizard of Oz* soundtrack or The Who's "Magic Bus" to extend the wizard theme.

• **"Wizard, Wizard, Warlock."** (Play this just like "Duck, Duck, Goose"—younger kids never get tired of it!)

A Real Fixer-Upper

For the child who lives to tear your house apart, round up the crew and put together a cool construction party. Need a blueprint for the bash? It's easy: Just build anticipation, break open the toolbox, and let 'em go to work.

INVITATIONS

Invite by the Inch

Hand out invitations that more than measure up by printing the details on the back of plain wooden rulers. Use a permanent marker to write a message on the ruler, or employ a small computer font and tape this printed message to the back of the ruler.

DECORATIONS

Tooling Around

Construction parties that allow for real tools and building fun are best held in a basement or garage. Create an authentic construction zone by hanging yellow and orange poster-

(continued on page 44)

> Help Mike build his birthday party from the ground up on Saturday, October 5, from 12:00 P.M. to 2:00 P.M. Bring a hammer and your appetite: Cake, ice cream, and a fix-yer-own sandwich buffet await. The Jones construction site is located at 1234 Maple Lane. RSVP 555-1234.

PARTY ZONE!

(continued from page 42)

board signs that read, "Kids at Work," "Bulldozer Crossing," or "Beware: Hard Hat Area." For extra fun, you may want to create a blueprint of a birthday party. Draw it up as if it was a house with different rooms, but instead of writing room names like "kitchen" or "dining room," write different activities, such as "Construction Junction," "Tool Time," and "Make It or Break It." Title the blueprint "(Child's Name)'s Birthday Party," and hang it on the wall.

Yellow "caution" tape and colored pylon cones are available at many local hardware stores. Run a few lengths of caution tape along the walkway leading up to the front door, and position pylons in and around the play area. Toy trucks and construction vehicles lend just the right ambience, and blinking yellow, red, or white Christmas lights complete the "danger" zone. Stretch lengths of orange fencing to keep kids out of off-limit areas.

FAVORS
Favor Fix

Create a kid's tool kit by packing tools like mini screwdrivers, wrenches, tape measures, pencils, and levels into the pockets of a canvas waist smock, then roll the smock up. Secure each tool roll-up with a yellow caution-tape bow. (You usually can find these tools at a dollar store or other inexpensive odds-and-ends shop. Check the paint department of your local hardware store for inexpensive waist smocks.) For younger kids, try toy versions of these tools, along with miniature construction vehicles and toy trucks.

Tool Time

Kids love to pound, hammer, and create! For older children, set out a few boards and wood scraps, safety goggles, and a box of nails, and let the kids dig into the construction site with all their might—just make sure there's plenty of adult supervision! For younger children, set up a construction site with toy tools, trucks, and construction vehicles.

Make It or Break It

To engineer some fun for the construction-savvy crowd, pick up a load of small, thick pieces of scrap wood (about the size of children's playing blocks) at the hardware store. Arrange the kids in a circle around the scrap pile. Pick one larger piece of wood and lay it on the floor to start. Each child will then take turns balancing a piece of wood on top of the previously placed piece. Although the objective is to keep the tower from toppling, younger kids enjoy the crash most of all!

Other Games

• **Nail it:** Turn "Pin the Tail on the Donkey" on its head with a game of "Hit the Nail on the Head." Draw a large nail in the center of a piece of poster board. Surround it with cutouts or drawings of items that will cause giggles when "hit": eggs, silly faces, alarm clocks, or balloons. Give each guest a construction paper hammer, write their name on it, and stick a piece of double-sided tape on the back. One at a time, blindfold each guest, spin them around gently, and let them take their best shot. Encourage the other kids to shout out sounds when the wrong objects are hit: Suggest "Splat!" for the egg, "Ouch!" for the face, and "Pop!" for the balloon.

• **Cover all:** Working construction is a dirty job and somebody's got to do it, but not without dressing for the job! Gather the following adult-size clothes (two sets of each): large work pants (Mom or Dad's paint-splattered Saturday jeans work great), work shirts, hats, belts, and boots. Make

two piles of clothes, and divide the kids into two teams. The teams will race to pull the work clothes on over their clothes (one person at a time) with their teammates' help. When fully dressed, the child runs to a

predetermined place and then back to the team, where he or she strips all the work clothes off and passes them to the next teammate to repeat the process. The team that finishes first wins.

• **Ruler relay:** When you buy the wooden rulers for the invitations, get a few extra for relay races around the yard. Using the rulers as they would a track baton, the children circle the house or run a zany path on their way back to the start/baton-exchange point.

Construction Junction

After a hard day on the job, kids deserve a treat bigger and sweeter than anything a lunch pail could offer. Reward your tool timers with this yummy construction-site cake.

1 (13×9-inch) cake
1 (14×10-inch) cake board, covered
2 cans (16 ounces each) chocolate frosting
1 cup crushed chocolate cookies
$\frac{1}{2}$ cup graham cracker crumbs
    Peanut creme patties
    Plain breadsticks
    Dark chocolate nuggets
    Small bear-shape graham cookies
    Assorted-color decorator gels

1. Trim top and sides of cake. Place on prepared cake board.

2. Frost entire cake with chocolate frosting.

3. Sprinkle crushed cookies over portions of cake to resemble dirt. Arrange graham cracker crumbs to resemble road.

4. Create building using peanut creme patties, breadsticks, and chocolate nuggets as shown in photo. Decorate bear-shape cookies to resemble construction workers; arrange bears and toys around construction site.

Makes 16 to 20 servings

Fix-Yer-Own Sandwich Buffet

Construction workers need to refuel with something quick, tasty, and easy to eat on-site. Before the lunch whistle blows (try it, they'll love it!), set out a few stacks of lunch meats, cheese, and breads so they can build their own hero. Or, for an even easier alternative, set out hot dogs with all the fixins. An overturned hard hat filled with treats—think PayDay candy bars, beef jerky, Big League chewing gum—is worth its weight in steel.

47

Kings and Queens for a Day

Don't let your child's birthday party be a royal pain—let it be royal! Throwing a gala in the grand tradition of Camelot is easy: Just make your birthday child king or queen for the day, welcome a court of guests, and use these great ideas to turn the celebration into an event no noble will forget.

INVITATIONS

Ye Olde Invites

Find parchment paper at a local art supply or craft store, or send today's typing paper back to the Middle Ages by wiping some sheets with a sponge dipped in lemon juice, then slipping them, for just a minute or two, into a warm oven. (Tip: If you overbake your stationery, try pressing a damp paper towel to the back of the paper.)

Once the paper is yellowed but not crisp (you'll need to roll it later), write the party details in a fancy script or use a calligraphic computer font. Roll each sheet into a scroll, and tie with a purple or gold bow.

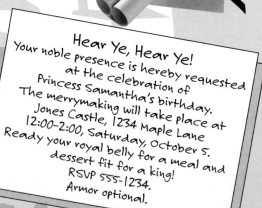

Hear Ye, Hear Ye!
Your noble presence is hereby requested at the celebration of Princess Samantha's birthday. The merrymaking will take place at Jones Castle, 1234 Maple Lane 12:00–2:00, Saturday, October 5. Ready your royal belly for a meal and dessert fit for a king! RSVP 555-1234. Armor optional.

dragons and unicorns. A banner that reads "King (Child's Name)'s Castle" makes a special finishing touch for the entryway.

Crowning Glory

An exciting craft is just what the alchemist ordered to jump-start the party. Have a craft table ready with silk, dried, or even fresh-cut wildflowers; ribbon; faux gems; glue; crayons or markers; and poster board already cut into crown shapes. (Keep tape or a stapler handy to fasten the flat crowns into a circle after they have been decorated.) Invite the kids to decorate a crown, or, if they prefer a crowning wreath, show them how to twist flowers into a circle using wired ribbon or floral wire.

Surely You Joust

For a rousing modern twist on an old favorite, hold a game of licorice joust. Pair the kids up in teams of two. Give a licorice stick (the length of a straw) to one member of each team, and give a mini bagel to each of the remaining members. Have the kids with bagels wedge them under their chin so the holes

DECORATIONS

Decorations That Rule

Extravagance has never been so easy. To doll up your castle with a lavish and lush look, go for purple and gold balloons and streamers. Hang twisted streamers from the center of the ceiling to the edges of the room for a tented ballroom effect, and allow balloons to fall where they may.

A purple tablecloth scattered with foil-wrapped chocolate coins and set with a few regal plastic goblets (find them at the party store) looks majestic. A bowl brimming with grapes, oranges, and apples makes for a royal centerpiece.

Trim the castle walls with poster board cutouts of flags, shields, or crests decorated with vibrant colors and pictures of face forward; the kids with the licorice should have one end of the licorice in their mouths.

With both hands behind their backs, the teams must "joust" the licorice "sword" into the bagel's center. Because the licorice tends to be a little limp and floppy, some silly dance moves may ensue; be ready with a video camera. Reward whichever team succeeds first with special badges of honor (stickers) to affix to their respective crowns.

It will please the court immensely if you offer up some other amusements that never get olde. Some to try:

• **Charades:** Use simple and common objects, words, and phrases as the words in question for young players, and be sure to remind the kids how to show simple clues (two fingers equals two words, a tug on the ear means "sounds like," and a strikeout sign means "start over").

• **Crouching knight:** Set two fat telephone books about five feet apart, and have a guest crouch down on each. Give each "crouching knight" one end of a rope that reaches the distance between them, and have them

grip tightly with both hands. The object is to pull hard enough to make the other knight fall off—without losing their own balance. This game takes a lot of skill!

FAVORS

Crown Jewels

Fill a velvet or satin sack with foil-wrapped chocolate coins, tops, candy rings, faux gems, plastic costume jewelry, or ornate initial stamps and colorful ink pads.

Let Them Eat Cake

Marie Antoinette had the right idea if she was talking about a dessert as sweet as this castle cake.

5½ cups cake batter, divided
1 (15×15-inch) cake board, covered, or large platter
2 cans (16 ounces each) white frosting
Food coloring
4 sugar ice cream cones
50 chocolate-covered wafer cookies
9 square dark chocolate mints
Assorted candies, decors, and fruit rollups

1. Preheat oven to 350°F. Grease and flour 9-inch square cake pan and medium muffin pan. Pour 3½ cups cake batter into cake pan; pour remaining cake batter into muffin cups (¼ cup batter per muffin cup). Bake cake in pan 35 to 45 minutes and cupcakes about 20 minutes or until toothpick inserted into centers comes out clean. Cool 15 minutes in pans. Loosen edges; invert onto wire racks and cool completely.

2. Trim top and sides of square cake and tops of 4 cupcakes. (Reserve remaining cupcakes for another use.) Place cake on prepared cake board. Place 1 cupcake upside down on each corner of cake; attach with small amount of frosting.

3. Tint 1 can frosting pink. Divide second can of frosting in half; tint half yellow and half purple.

4. Frost entire cake and cupcakes with pink frosting. Frost ice cream cones with yellow frosting.

5. Place frosted cones on top of cupcakes. Using medium writing tip and purple frosting, pipe decorative lines around tops and bottoms of cones, cupcakes, and square cake.

6. Place chocolate wafer cookies around sides of cake, alternating whole cookies with cookies cut down by one fourth to create castle wall. Decorate castle with assorted candies, cookies, decors, and fruit rollups cut into flag shapes.

Makes 14 to 16 servings

The Feast

Since forks weren't invented in time for medieval eatin', serve authentic finger fare like turkey drumsticks (chicken drumsticks will do for smaller folk), a slurpy soup drunk straight from the bowl, and a loaf of unsliced bread torn to shreds. Kids will revel in the opportunity to get touchy-feely with their food, and on a special day like this one, there's no reason to encourage them to do otherwise. Serve apple cider to wash it all down—and be thankful goblets were available!

Bug Out

What has 16 legs, 8 heads, and frosting all over its 80 fingers? Your favorite bug's next birthday party, of course! Ride the wings of your child's insect insanity, and make flying, fuzzy, and creepy-crawly creatures the feature of this year's birthday celebration.

INVITATIONS

What's the Buzz?

Get the guests' antennae twitching with these adorable insect invitations—choose beetles or ladybugs. They couldn't be easier: All you need is some poster board and metal brads.

1. Trace a CD onto red or black poster board, and cut out. For each beetle invitation, cut 2 black circles. Cut 1 of these circles in half. (The halves will be the bug wings.) For ladybugs, cut out 1 red circle and 1 black circle for each invitation. Cut the red circle in half for wings.

2. On the full circles, write the party particulars in silver ink. Or, find a funky computer font, and print out the information on white paper. Cut the paper to fit, and glue it onto the front of the full circles.

(continued on page 56)

What's the buzz?
Jamie is turning 8!
Buzz on over to the Jones's colony at
1234 Maple Lane
to help Jamie celebrate.
When: Saturday, October 5,
12:00–2:00
Cake, ice cream, and a picnic
lunch will be served.
RSVP: 555-1234

54

(continued from page 54)

3. Place 2 circle halves on top of each full circle. Press a metal brad through the top of both wings and the circle underneath. The wings will twist open and shut over the text.

4. Cut a small crescent out of black poster board for each invitation, and glue it to the top of the bug to create a head.

5. Decorate the head and wings as you like.

DECORATIONS

Insect Kingdom

Hang green crepe paper in the entranceway, and invite guests into the world that lives under the leaves: Turn standing lamps into giant plants by taping green poster board or craft-foam leaves along their stems. Do the same to ceiling fans and tabletop lamps. If you feel it's safe, haul houseplants into the area. Tape green streamers to the ceiling in long strips, making sure to leave space above the kids' heads for jumping and reaching room. Finally, sprinkle plastic ants, ladybugs, and other insects over tables. Background music of forest sounds or crickets chirping will help kids dig in to the earthy feel.

Make way for a bug's feast by covering the table with a red-and-white checkered tablecloth. Or, for a pest-itively wonderful look, put it on the floor! The kids will love the unexpected surprise of casual picnic dining.

FAVORS

Bug Bag

Keep kids busy from the minute they walk in the door by handing them a goodie bag filled with tools for a successful bug hunt: a plastic magnifying glass, a small screen bug house or small jar with holes already punched in the lid, and a bug-catching net. Don't forget to provide field food snacks like chocolate bugs, gummy worms, and insect fruit snacks, too! Let the kids loose in the yard if you can—making sure they understand all bugs need to be left outdoors—or unleash the guests in the party room among the plastic bugs.

GAMES/ACTIVITIES

Search Party

Dab a dot of nail polish on the bellies—ahem, abdomens—of several plastic insects, then plant them under "leaves," on

ledges, and around the playroom before the guests arrive. When the time is right for a challenge, tell the kids to grab their magnifying glasses and begin a search for the painted-belly bugs!

Web of Ties

Before the party, buy one skein of yarn, each a different color, for each guest. (For older kids, buy several multicolor skeins.) The day of the party, tie a prize to the loose end of each ball, and while the guests are filling up on eats in another room, have an adult helper or two hide the prizes in various locations such as under sofa cushions, behind a book, on a side table (*not* inside the door of your china cabinet!). With the hidden prize as the anchor, unravel the yarn while criss-crossing the room and the other lengths of yarn. When a mixed-up web forms, cut the yarn free from the skein, and call the kids

in. Let each choose a piece of yarn, and tell everyone to untangle their way to a prize. Kids of all ages love rolling around on the floor, tiptoeing through the strands, and twisting around each other to escape the web.

Another option to consider is setting up the maze before the party so it can be the kids' first activity.

The Great Outdoors... and Indoors

If you're lucky enough to have warm weather, an afternoon outdoors armed with insect-finding tools is probably enough to keep the kids buzzing with activity. But should you need some other ideas, consider:

• **"Tick" Tock:** For young kids, a buggy name twist on the old favorite, "What Time Is It, Mr. Clock?"

• **Spiderman:** A basic game of tag, with "it" being the preda-

tor spider and the hunted "flies" being dinner.

• **Metamorphosis portraits:** Delight your guests by giving them a chance to fly. How? Simply draw a colorful butterfly on one side of a white poster board. Where the butterfly's head would be, cut out a hole big enough for a child's face. On the other side, draw a dragonfly with the hole where the "face" would be. Let the kids pick which they want to be, then have a helper hold up the board while each child sticks their face through. Zoom into the frame so the surrounding walls don't show, and snap an instant photo for the kids to take home.

REFRESHMENTS

Bug Bites

Don't just serve sandwiches for lunch—catch kids in a web of excitement by turning sandwiches into edible *insectwiches*! Cut sandwiches into rectangular thirds. Stick olives or grapes on toothpicks and insert them into one end of the sandwich for eyes. Cut two 1-inch slits in the top of the bread, and press in small lettuce leaf wings. Want

legs? Poke a few carrot or celery sticks out the sides. For once, kids won't want to play with their food; they'll prefer to dissect it!

Waiter, There's a Bug in My Drink!

A few days before the party, drop gummy insects or worms into ice cube trays filled with water, and freeze. Serve in a glass of clear soda or lemonade. Kids will go buggy when they see what's hiding in their drink!

Bee Sweet

Take the sting out of boring birthday cakes by serving up "Stripes" with a side of sorbet.

    4 cups cake batter
    1 (10-inch) round cake board, covered, or large plate
    1¾ cups prepared white frosting
        Food coloring
        Assorted black, yellow, and red candies
        Black licorice twists

1. Preheat oven to 350°F. Grease and flour 2½-quart ovenproof bowl. Pour cake batter into prepared bowl. Bake 60 to 70 minutes or until wooden skewer inserted into center comes out clean. Cool 15 minutes in bowl. Loosen edge; invert onto wire rack and cool completely.

2. Trim flat side of cake. Turn cake over, and cut small piece from top of cake to slightly flatten back of bee, if desired. Place cake on prepared cake board.

3. Reserve ¼ cup white frosting. Tint ¾ cup frosting black and ¾ cup frosting yellow.

4. Using toothpick, mark semicircle about 3½ inches from 1 edge of cake for face and 3 parallel semicircles for rest of body.

5. Frost face with reserved white frosting. Alternately frost body sections with yellow and black, piping frosting with floral tip to create fuzzy texture, if desired. Reserve small portion of black frosting for piping.

6. Using medium writing tip and reserved black frosting, pipe line between head and body.

7. Arrange assorted candies and licorice twists for face, antennae, legs, wings, and stinger as shown in photo.

Makes 14 to 18 servings

Party Like a Rock Star

You'll never mention all the times you've caught your so-called "shy" child singing into a hairbrush in the bathroom, but you can help bring the house down just the same. This birthday, turn your home into a stage and invite a band of the birthday star's best friends over to rock 'n' roll. It's guaranteed to start off this new year on a high note!

INVITATIONS

Mike Up

Give kids an in to the hippest party in town by creating a simple back-stage pass.

Cut construction paper or colored poster board into squares (1 for each invitation), and draw a special design on 1 side and write the party information on the back. For an official look, have the passes laminated at a copy store, or simply place them between the sticky sides of 2 sheets of clear adhesive paper and cut. Use a hole puncher to make a

Backstage Pass

Admit one: to Laura's rockin' birthday bash

Venue: 1234 Maple Lane

Pass valid: 12:00 – 2:00

Saturday, October 5

Contact: 555-1234 for RSVP

(continued on page 64)

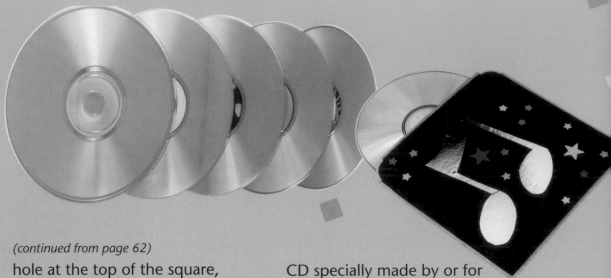

(continued from page 62)

hole at the top of the square, and thread a piece of sparkly cording through so the pass can be worn as a necklace.

DECORATIONS
Music in the Air

Let the party room suit your child's star style. Hang posters of the kids' favorite stars, and add to the effect by hand-painting signs that scream "I Love Joey" or "Jessica Rules!"

Buy blank CDs in bulk, and suspend them from the ceiling. Spinning CDs create a cool disco-ball lighting effect. Speaking of disco balls . . . pick one up at your local party store and hang it prominently in the party room. Look for a table-cloth or place settings decorated with musical notes—they're easy to find. Rock out to a mix

CD specially made by or for the birthday child.

GAMES/ACTIVITIES
CD Sleeves

If you've burned a special party soundtrack, let the guests personalize their own CD sleeves. Before the party, cut pieces of tagboard big enough to hold a CD (2 pieces for each disc). Use craft glue to attach 2 pieces together—gluing only on 3 sides so there's a place for the CD to slide in and out. (Make sure the sleeves are still big enough to hold a CD once the pieces of cardboard are glued together.) Allow plenty of time for the glue to dry. At the party, provide glitter, glue, ribbons, markers, stickers, and foil so the kids can personalize their CD sleeves.

Video Vixens

Few things are as entertaining to kids as seeing themselves on TV. Give them a step up the ladder to small-screen stardom by providing makeup, hair accessories, and glitzy costumes, and let 'em transform themselves into rock stars. Provide faux microphones and instruments for the rockers to use as props, and when they're ready to take the stage and rock out, videotape them creating a music video.

Star Performance

If the kids ever tire of retakes and reviews, these star-studded games and activities will keep them busy:

• **Name that tune:** Make a list of lyrics from oldies as well as Top 40 hits, and see how many the guests can identify.

• **Musical chairs:** An oldie but a goodie, as far as younger children are concerned. No rockin' party can be without it.

Star Necessities

There are certain things a rock star just cannot be without, so load up the goodie bags with the following loot: sunglasses (find inexpensive ones at party stores or dollar stores), a CD burned with the special birthday mix soundtrack so the party can go on and on, an autograph book, earplugs, and music-themed toys or candy.

Concert Concessions

Typical concert fare is fabulous. Serve pizza by the slice, soda, popcorn, or soft pretzels. Most likely, the guests' jaws will be flapping to the music that's playing, so keep lunch at a snack bar, serve-yourself style.

Microphone Mania

With music blasting in the background, they may not hear you when you yell, "Let's cut the cake!" But that's what birthday candles are for. Once you've got their attention, keep it with these mouthwatering renditions of miniature microphones.

1 package (18¼ ounces) white cake mix, plus ingredients
   to prepare mix
2 packages (12 cones each) colored flat-bottomed
   ice cream cones
1 can (16 ounces) white frosting
   Food coloring
   Candy-coated chocolate sprinkles and colored candy dots
24 (10-inch) licorice whips

1. Preheat oven to 350°F. Prepare cake mix according to package directions. Spoon about ¼ cup batter into each cone. Stand cones in 13×9-inch baking pan or on cookie sheets. (For easier handling, use pans with sides.)

2. Bake about 20 minutes or until toothpick inserted into center of cake comes out clean. Cool on wire racks.

3. Tint frosting desired colors; frost cones. Decorate with sprinkles and candy dots.

4. Poke hole in bottom of each cone with wooden skewer or tip of knife. Insert licorice whip into hole for microphone cord.

Makes 24 microphones

UNDER THE SEA

Don't leave your little fishy high and dry this birthday; throw an enchanting sea party. Awash in underwater scenery and island fun, this party looks fantastic from invite to end but takes minimal time and effort to pull together. The guests are sure to fall for it, hook, line, and sinker!

INVITATIONS

MESSAGE IN A BOTTLE

Fish for guests the old-fashioned way: Send each invitation as a message in a bottle. (Just don't expect an immediate RSVP unless you pass off the bottle to a delivery system more reliable than the high seas.) Making this invitation is simple. In the weeks before the party, save an empty plastic soda or water bottle (and cap) for each guest your child will invite.

Remove the labels from all the bottles, and write the party particulars on a piece of construction paper or kraft paper. Add to the castaway feel of the invitations by tearing the edges of the paper. Roll up each note, and tie with a

AHOY MATES!
Jessie is turning 7. Cruise over to 1234 Maple Lane on Sat., Oct. 5 for a celebration under the sea. We'll descend to the depths at 12:00 and rise to the surface at 2:00. Lunch, cake, and fun are on deck. Are you? RSVP: 555-1234

(continued on page 70)

(continued from page 68)

bow of green yarn or raffia "seaweed." Keep one end of the yarn long enough to dangle out of the bottle's opening for easy retrieval. Slip the scroll in, screw the cap back on to keep the yarn from slipping in. Happy sailing ... er, delivering.

20,000 LEAGUES UNDER THE SEA

A little goes a long way when it comes to ocean decorations. Here's a freshwater idea: Start with blue crepe paper streamers twisted and hung in waves across the ceiling. For seaweed, intersperse the waves with dangling green streamers. Hang one or both of the colors in the doorways.

Along the walls, tape pictures—homemade, clipped from magazines, or store bought—of fish, seahorses, starfish, an octopus, and even a shark or two. If you have a soccer net or hammock that's

not in use, toss it over the sofa or another large piece of furniture. Don't forget to play a CD of whale calls or crashing waves; it'll breathe a lot of life into your aquatic scene. For a final touch, hang a disco ball in the center of the ceiling and give it a spin. The thousands of twirling reflectors will dapple your sea walls with a beautiful light the kids will love.

MOTION OF THE OCEAN

For a cool craft project, teach your school of fish how to re-create the motion of the ocean in a jar. All you need is blue food coloring, water, clear baby oil, a spoon, a few trinkets, and one widemouthed container for each guest (empty plastic juice bottles or baby food jars work great).

Help each child fill their container halfway with water.

Squeeze a drop (or two, for bigger bottles) of blue food coloring into each bottle, and instruct the kids to stir it into the water. Drop in a few small trinkets such as shells, plastic fish, boats, or a treasure chest, and then add baby oil until the bottle is filled almost to the top. Wipe off any drips, and cap each bottle tightly.

To be certain curious hands won't open the bottles, line the inner rim of each cap with a few drops of super glue or liquid cement before screwing on the cap (an adult's job!). Make sure to wipe up any glue drips to prevent sticky finger nightmares.

Because oil and water won't mix, when the children shake and tilt the container they'll see the liquid undulating like waves in the ocean.

MAKE A SPLASH

Keep the party swimming with games like these:

• **Go fish:** There's rarely a kid who doesn't know how to play this game, but they've all got their own set of rules. Make sure everyone agrees how the game is played before handing out the card decks.

• **Go fish . . . for real:** Well, OK, not completely real, but lure them in just the same by handing out "fishing rods" (empty wrapping paper tubes with fishing line or string and a large paperclip bent into a hook at the end of each line). On the floor, scatter dry dish sponges cut into the shape of fish. Each sponge fish should have a large paperclip (still in its original paperclip shape) hooked through its mouth. Let the kids take turns casting and "hooking" their fish from a few feet away. (Keep onlookers a safe distance away. The only things you want the kids to hook are the fish!)

• **Treasures of the deep:** Before the party, spray-paint a bunch of pennies gold (or use fake gold coins). While the kids are eating lunch, scatter the gold coins in different hiding places throughout the backyard or party room. When they're ready to hunt for Blackbeard's gold, show the kids an example of the hidden coins, then turn them loose.

FAVORS

SEA SATCHELS

All seafarers fare far better than landlubbers when armed with a sea

satchel full of sea essentials. (Try saying that seven times!) Bestow upon each guest a pirate's booty: a fishnet sack filled with fish-shape snack crackers, Swedish Fish candy, a fishing bobber, toy boats, fish stickers, mermaid paraphernalia, or even bath bubbles.

DESSERT ISLAND

Need a dessert you won't desert? Try this easy island cake!

- 1 (13×9-inch) cake
- 1 (14×10-inch) cake board, covered
- 1 can (16 ounces) white frosting
- Food coloring
- 1½ cups graham cracker crumbs
- 6 green gumdrops
- 1 pretzel rod, broken in half
- Small bear-shape graham cookies
- Assorted decorator gels (optional)
- Assorted candies and goldfish crackers

1. Trim top and sides of cake. Place on prepared cake board.

2. Tint frosting blue.

3. Frost entire cake with blue frosting. Spoon graham cracker crumbs onto frosting to resemble island.

4. Flatten gumdrops with rolling pin on smooth, flat surface or sheet of waxed paper sprinkled with sugar. Roll until very thin (about ¹⁄₁₆ inch), turning frequently to coat with sugar. Cut each gumdrop into leaf shape with sharp knife or scissors. Position pretzel rod near center of island; attach leaves to top of pretzel with frosting to form palm tree, as shown in photo.

5. Decorate bear-shape cookies with decorator gels, if desired. Arrange bear-shape cookies, candies, and goldfish crackers on cake.

Makes 16 to 20 servings

KNOCKOUT PUNCH

For a punch with bite, make a batch of blue fruit punch and pour it into clear cups filled with Swedish Fish candy. Don't forget straws: Kids love to stir the fish into a whirlpool swim.

DINO-MITE!

Dinosaurs may be extinct, but prehistoric parties never get old—they just get easier! To create a land before time that no birthdaysaurus will ever forget, uncover these recipes and activities. They're inexpensive, inventive, and best of all, require no stone tools or fire-building skills.

INVITATIONS

DINO DELIVERY

A dinosaur-egg invitation makes for an extra-special delivery!

1. Sketch or trace small dinosaur shapes onto construction paper (1 for each invitation). Cut out.

2. Write the details of the party on each dinosaur.

3. Roll the dinosaur up, and stretch the lip of a white balloon (medium or large ones stretch better) so you can slip the invitation inside.

4. Blow up the balloon only ¼ full so it won't pop easily, then knot it.

Calling all herbivores and carnivores!
Stamp, stalk or swoop over to Kevin's birthdaysaurus bash.
He's 10 years old (almost a dinosaur himself!) and
ready to dig up some Jurassic fun.
WHEN: Saturday, October 5, 11:00-1:00
WHERE: Jones' swamp (1234 Maple Lane)
WHAT: Dinosaur cake and bones will be unearthed.
RSVP: 555-1234

(continued on page 76)

(continued from page 74)

5. Nestle each "egg" atop some craft grass inside a small box. (You can find both at most craft stores.) On the outside of the box, write "Open at Your Own Risk" and "Do Not Feed!" The egg is ready for delivery!

DECORATIONS

ROMP IN THE SWAMP

If you thought your house was a jungle before, get ready to take it to the next level. Bring guests to the murky depths of the Mesozoic era by hanging green crepe paper from the ceiling and doorframes. Pull your potted plants into the party room, and cut green felt or craft foam to make dinosaur footprints leading up to the house or from room to room. The *Jurassic Park* soundtrack completes the ambience.

GAMES/ACTIVITIES

FOSSIL FIND

In good weather, bury plastic dinosaur toys in an outdoor sandbox for excavation. If the great outdoors aren't an option, mix up some simple "fossilized" salt clay before the party.

In a large bowl, mix together 2 cups all-purpose flour, 1 cup salt, 1 cup cold tea or coffee, 2 tablespoons cooking oil, and a handful of wet coffee grounds. (Estimate 1 batch for every 2 kids.) Keep the dough covered until you're ready to use it.

Cover your table with a plastic cloth or newspaper. Invite the kids to knead and form the clay into dinosaur shapes or pound it into the shape of a rock and then press dinosaur-shape cookie cutters into the clay to make their own fossils. Bake 1 hour at 300°F to fossilize these rocks!

Prehistoric Hysteria

For prehistoric twists on today's games, consider:

• **Dinosaur dancing:** Arrange a circle of chairs—one less chair than there are play-ers—facing inward. Assign the name of a dinosaur to each child, and choose one child to be IT. That person stands in the center of the circle and calls out the names of two dinosaurs. Those two "dinosaurs" must race to switch seats before IT gets to either of their chairs.

If IT yells "Dinosaurs dance!" all players must race to find new seats. The person left standing is the new IT.

• **Who am I?:** If you're willing to do a little homework, make up a list of several features that separate one dinosaur from another. Give these hints as clues until the kids can guess which dinosaur you're talking about.

• **Mummy wrap:** Do the "time wrap" again by dividing the kids into teams of two. Give each team a roll of toilet paper.

One person is the wrapper; the other is the mummy. The wrappers must wrap their mummies in toilet paper from head to toe as quickly as possible. If they move too fast and the toilet paper breaks, they must start again. The first team to complete the task without breaking the toilet paper wins.

FAVORS

BAG O' BONES

Hand out small plastic buckets crammed with all the tools the guests will need for an archaeological dig: a plastic shovel for digging, a small paintbrush for dusting the bones clean, a plastic magnifying glass, a small plastic or stuffed dinosaur toy, and more!

A BONE TO PICK

*Make no bones about it, dinosaur-bone meringue treats
make quite a decorative feast.*

4 egg whites, at room temperature
½ teaspoon cream of tartar
1 cup powdered sugar
1 teaspoon vanilla extract

1. Preheat oven to 200°F. Line cookie sheets with parchment paper; set aside.

2. Beat egg whites in small bowl until foamy.

3. Gradually add cream of tartar, then sugar; continue beating until stiff peaks form.

4. Fold in vanilla.

5. Transfer mixture to small plastic resealable food storage bag, and cut off 1 corner. Pipe onto prepared cookie sheets in the shape of bones.

6. Bake 1 hour (do not let tops brown). Turn oven off; leave bones in oven with door closed 1 more hour or just until dry. Cool completely; carefully remove from cookie sheets. Store in airtight container up to 1 week.

Place a couple of bones around the cake before you serve it; wrap individual bones in waxed paper to sweeten the goodie bag booty; or set bowls of bones around the party room.

EGG 'EM ON

When it comes time to feed your carnivores, zap dinosaur eggs into the 21st century by popping mini pizza rolls in the microwave and serving them in a nest...er, bowl lined with ripped up pieces of brown paper bags. Toss a few sticks (chopsticks, that is!) on top. Besides looking like a cool nest of dinosaur eggs, the presentation serves a purpose as well: Kids can use the chopsticks to spear their pizza rolls, and the paper bags will absorb drips and grease.

DINO DESSERT

Cave moms never had it so easy! Slay this dinosaur cake for your cave kids, and prepare to be bigger than the invention of fire.

1 (13×9-inch) cake
1 (14×10-inch) cake board, covered, or large platter
2¼ cups prepared white frosting
Food coloring
Assorted hard candies and gumdrops

1. Trim top and sides of cake. Using Diagram 1 as guide, draw stegosaurus pattern on 13×9-inch piece of waxed paper. Cut pattern out, and place on cake. Cut out dinosaur; place on prepared cake board. Attach piece A to piece B, as shown in Diagram 2, using small amount of frosting.

2. Reserve ¼ cup frosting. Tint remaining frosting dark purple.

3. Frost entire cake with purple frosting.

4. Using medium writing tip and reserved white frosting, pipe outline of dinosaur and body parts as shown in photo.

5. Decorate dinosaur with candies as shown in photo.

Makes 12 to 16 servings

Diagram 1

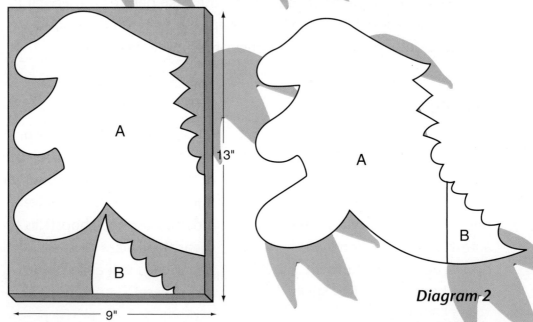

13"

9"

Diagram 2

In the Stars

Remember when your parents used to tell you they hoped you would have a child just like yourself one day? Looks like you've made your date with destiny! Honor fate's full circle and the birthday of the child for whom you were destined by throwing a celestial celebration that shines brighter than the stars themselves—no planet alignment necessary.

Present for the Future

In the weeks before the party, have your child find out the birthdate of each guest you plan to invite. The invitations will be each guest's personal "horoscope."

Cut purple construction paper into squares (1 for each invitation). At the top of each square, write the guest's name and astrological sign, followed by the details of the party. (If your child doesn't find out the guests' birthdays in time, don't sweat it. The invitation works just as well without them: Just omit the child's sign from the top.) Fold each invitation in half and in

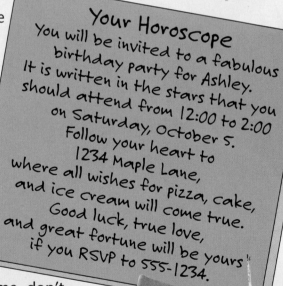

Your Horoscope
You will be invited to a fabulous birthday party for Ashley. It is written in the stars that you should attend from 12:00 to 2:00 on Saturday, October 5. Follow your heart to 1234 Maple Lane, where all wishes for pizza, cake, and ice cream will come true. Good luck, true love, and great fortune will be yours if you RSVP to 555-1234.

(continued on page 84)

82

Read
your
Fortune

(continued from page 82)
half again. For an added touch, sprinkle a small dusting of silver sparkles on the invite before folding. Finish the "present"-ation by tying a silver bow around each square.

DECORATIONS

Ribbons in the Sky

Want your kid to go on believing you hung the moon? Well then, go ahead and hang it! The theme of this party is mystical and magical. Translation? Moons and stars are the stuff birthday party dreams are made of. Affix glow-in-the-dark stars to the ceiling and walls, or hang a mix of aluminum foil–covered cardboard stars and colored ribbons from the ceiling. Curl the ribbons into spirals by dragging the sharp edge of a scissor blade along each length.

The outlook is good for fun fortune telling if you hang strings of beads in open door-ways or just the front entrance, and use a Magic 8-Ball toy or crystal ball as a table center-piece. Don't have one? Don't fret. Rinse out the inside of a round glass bowl, blow a hand-ful of glitter inside so it sticks to the damp sides, and then turn it over on the table. Voilà! A crystal ball!

For the ultimate in dream-scape design, play meditation or relaxation music featuring a harp or another ethereal sound. A vase of petaled flowers, such as daisies, will complete the heavenly atmosphere—and provide everything the girls will need to keep busy with a quick

84

round of "he loves me, he loves me not" while you serve lunch.

Special Guest

If you've got a friend or relative willing to don a headscarf, hoop earrings, and a pile of clinking bracelets, you've got yourself a fortune-teller. Dim the lights, burn some incense or a candle, and set up a small covered table for your teller. Allow each guest to sit before the fortune-teller and have their palms read or fortunes told while the other guests sit nearby. Having the guests as an audience keeps the scene from seeming too spooky and keeps everyone interested.

The teller should be ready with plenty of positive forecasts—and some silly predictions to get the giggles rolling. Consider:

"I see you inventing something very exciting . . ."

"You have a special talent. Animals seem to understand you and trust you because you're careful and gentle. Have you ever considered being a veterinarian?"

"When you think you have met your true love, you must dance the can-can while drinking a glass of soda. If the bubbles tickle your nose, he will be the one. If the bubbles come out your nose, he probably won't."

"I see 37 Baby . . . Ruths in your future. You had better be sure to brush after eating each one . . . or else I also see 37 cavities in your future."

Dream Catchers

For a fun activity, supply the girls with pretty ribbons, beads, feathers, chenille stems, and string so they can create their very own dream catchers. Follow these simple steps.

1. Bend a chenille stem into a small circle.

2. Twist a long piece of string or thin ribbon around the edges of the circle, and crisscross the circle several times to form a small web. This is the part that "catches" their dreams.

3. Decorate with ribbons, beads, and feathers.

Note: If your guests are under seven years old, it might be easier for you to do steps 1 and 2 yourself and let them decorate the dream catchers.

Fortune Fun

Obviously, every guest has hopes, dreams, and predictions of their own. Invite each guest to write theirs down for a birthday time capsule that will be opened at next year's party.

If they can't wait that long to find out if their predictions will come true, here are some great games to keep them guessing in the meantime:

• **Apple of my eye:** Give each guest an apple with a stem. As they hold the stem between their index finger and thumb, have them twist the apple while reciting the alphabet (one twist per letter) until the stem breaks. The letter said when the stem breaks represents the first initial of their true love's name.

• **By a hair:** Distribute a plastic hair comb to each guest. Tell them to think of a question about their future that can be answered with a yes or no, and then, picking one tooth of the comb at random, tap from the far left tooth to the chosen tooth while reciting "yes, no, maybe so." Whichever word is said when the chosen tooth is reached is the answer.

• **See the future:** Before the party, use a toothpick or small paintbrush dipped in lemon juice to write words of fortune (wealth, success, good luck, happiness, and so on) on separate slips of paper. On one slip, write "winner." Put the slips in a cup, and allow each guest to draw one. Use kitchen tongs or tweezers to hold each slip of paper, one at a time, about an inch above a burning candle, being very careful not to burn the paper. (This is an adult's job!) As the paper warms, the words will appear. Reward the winner with a prize such as tarot cards or star stickers.

You're Getting Sleepy . . .

If the party is a sleepover, have each girl tie their big toe to another girl's big toe with thin thread before going to sleep. In the morning, check the broken thread. An old superstition says the girl with the longest thread piece will marry first.

FAVORS

Wish Sacks

Craft stores usually carry small satin or velvet bags. Fill them with take-no-chances items like fortune cookies, dice, individual horoscope rolls (these can be found near the check-out line at most drugstores or supermarkets), glitter pens, and mini notepads or diaries for recording dreams.

REFRESHMENTS

A Slice of Heaven

Planning a menu for kids is a gamble for anyone who isn't a professional medium, but odds are, pizza is a great bet. Order or make your own round pizza, then personalize it to the party's star-studded theme by cutting it in the shape of a star. The trimmed-away edges can be served as slices as well.

A Charming Snack

Stay true to the theme and your guests' taste buds by setting out small bowls of sweetened cereal with marshmallow charms—sans milk—for kids to snack on throughout the party.

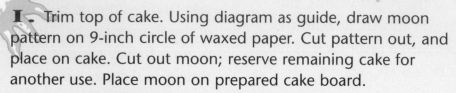

Moonlight Serenade

Follow up your brilliant pizza pie with more inspiration from the sky: a moon cake.

1 (9-inch) round cake
1 (10-inch) round cake board, covered, or large plate
1 can (16 ounces) white frosting
Food coloring
Red licorice whip

1. Trim top of cake. Using diagram as guide, draw moon pattern on 9-inch circle of waxed paper. Cut pattern out, and place on cake. Cut out moon; reserve remaining cake for another use. Place moon on prepared cake board.

2. Tint frosting yellow.

3. Frost entire cake with yellow frosting.

4. Create moon face with pieces of licorice, as shown in photo.

Makes 6 to 8 servings

FUN AT THE 50

Want to tackle a party that will leave everyone breathless? Drop and give 'em 50—the 50-yard line, that is! Football parties are simple to decorate, fun to host, and, if you can organize a peewee kickoff contest in the backyard, a riot to watch. Honor your lil' champion with a football fiesta, and watch the crowd go wild.

INVITATIONS
THE ROSTER

Use colored index cards or cut a piece of poster board into small rectangles with a notch at both ends to make sporting event "ticket" invitations. For an official look, paste copies of a picture that shows your child wearing a team uniform. Or, smear some grease-paint under their eyes (or use a black eyeliner), and snap away. Underneath, write a mini player bio. Write the party particulars on the back.

NAME: Jason Jones
HEIGHT: 3' 8"
WEIGHT: 56 lbs.
POSITION: Quarterback

Are you ready for some football?
Join the lineup at Jones' stadium in honor of
Jason's 7th birthday at
1234 Maple Lane
GAME DAY: Saturday, October 5
KICKOFF: Noon (until 2:00 p.m.)
HALFTIME: Lunch and cake will be served.
Please wear play clothes and get ready to rumble!
RSVP to Coach Jones at 555-1234

555 1212

DECORATIONS

STADIUM STUFF

Hang posters featuring your child's favorite teams and players, and decorate the party area with streamers and tableware in team colors. An overturned helmet filled with candy and trinkets makes a great centerpiece. Rely on marching band, university pep song, or "Jock Jams" CDs to pump up the players. In one corner of the kitchen (or outside, if weather permits), place plastic cups and a cooler filled with Gatorade thirst quenching drink. Just beware of an overenthusiastic team, Coach!

HUT, HUT, HIKE

Don't put a football in the house as a decoration unless you're willing to see your prized vase take its own "hike." Either leave footballs outside or employ a harmless foam football in an open indoor space.

CHAMPION ENTRY

Tape a large piece of butcher paper or a paper tablecloth (the color of your favorite team) to the frame of an open door. When it's showtime, turn up a marching band CD or fight song and let the kids burst through the paper like a real team about to take the field. Make bursting through the paper easier for little bruisers by cutting horizontal slits in the paper at head, waist, and foot level.

GAMES/ACTIVITIES

KICKOFF

Provide older kids with colored plastic sashes, and take them out to the backyard for a game of flag football. For younger kids, ditch the organized game in favor of some simple skill challenges. Let the kids take turns trying to kick, throw, and catch the football.

Stuck indoors? No problem. Kids of all ages love to watch and play paper football (a piece of notebook paper is folded into a tight triangle and "flicked" across a table into an opponent's circled arms). Warning: This can get rowdier than you'd think, so prepare to divert attention with other athletes' feats, such as

• **Silly shot put:** Kids spin around three times and then toss a paper plate as far as they can or, for more of a challenge, to specific targets marked by taped circles on the floor.

• **Weight lifter wunderkind:** Make "dumbbells" by attaching paper plates or foam "weights" to each end of a cardboard wrapping paper tube. Whoever gives the best dramatic performance wins.

• **Muddle huddle:** With parties of six or more, divide kids into two groups. Have each group get into a huddle, and use yarn to *loosely* tie each child's right ankle to the left ankle of the child to their right. Have the huddles race from one end of

the room to the other—without breaking the yarn! Kids have a blast falling all over each other, and it usually takes several tries before they balance well enough to keep the ties that bind intact.

FAVORS

ATHLETE'S ESSENTIALS

Instead of goodie bags, hand out sport bottles filled with Gatorade thirst quencher gum, energy bars, terrycloth wristbands, team trading cards, and chocolate sport ball candies.

SWEET VICTORY

Win one for the Gipper—and your little guy or gal—
with this gridiron cake.

1 (13×9-inch) cake
1 (14×10-inch) cake board, covered, or large platter
2 cups prepared white frosting
   Food coloring
   White decorator gel and other assorted colors
1 square (2 ounces) almond bark
2 pretzel rods
4 thin pretzel sticks
   Small bear-shape graham cookies

1. Trim top and sides of cake; place on prepared cake board.

2. Tint frosting medium green.

3. Frost entire cake with green frosting. Pipe field yardage lines with white decorator gel.

4. Melt almond bark in tall glass according to package directions. Break off one quarter of each pretzel rod; discard shorter pieces. Break 2 pretzel sticks in half. Dip pretzels in melted almond bark, turning to coat completely and tapping off excess. Using pretzel rods for support posts, pretzel sticks for crossbars, and pretzel stick halves for uprights, arrange pretzels in 2 goalpost formations on waxed paper; let dry completely. Carefully peel waxed paper from goalposts; set posts in each end of cake.

5. Meanwhile, decorate bear-shape cookies with decorator gels; position cookies throughout field as desired.

Makes 16 to 20 servings

TAILGATING

What's a football game without a tailgate spread? Beef up the team with typical tailgate fare like hot dogs, hamburgers, and potato chips. If the weather is right for a barbecue, go for extra yardage and spread stadium blankets on the lawn so the kids can chill while you grill. If you happen to have a pickup truck or SUV, drop the gate and use it for a true tailgate buffet!

TIME OUT

Ask an adult or sibling helper to be a stadium vendor. They can walk around with a box filled with licorice laces, individual peanut sacks, or bags of popcorn (or a combination of all these treats), calling out—what else?—"Candy! Peanuts! Popcorn! Get 'em here!"